BRIGHT IDEA BOOKS

A Plant THAT EATS Spiders AND OTHER COOL GREEN-AND-GROWING FACTS

by Kaitlyn Duling

Content Consultant

Jeff Conner, PhD
Professor of Plant Biology
Michigan State University

CAPSTONE PRESS
a capstone imprint

Bright Idea Books are published by Capstone Press
1710 Roe Crest Drive, North Mankato, Minnesota 56003
www.mycapstone.com

Library of Congress Cataloging-in-Publication Data
Names: Duling, Kaitlyn, author.
Title: A plant that eats spiders and other cool green-and-growing facts / by Kaitlyn Duling.
Description: North Mankato, Minnesota : Capstone Press, [2019] | Includes
   bibliographical references and index.
Identifiers: LCCN 2018035981 | ISBN 9781543557718 (hardcover : alk. paper) |
   ISBN 9781543558036 (ebook)
Subjects: LCSH: Plants--Juvenile literature.
Classification: LCC QK49 .D725 2019 | DDC 581--dc23
LC record available at https://lccn.loc.gov/2018035981

Editorial Credits
Editor: Meg Gaertner
Designer: Becky Daum
Production Specialist: Colleen McLaren

Photo Credits
iStockphoto: Boogich, 25, eefauscan, 20–21, javarman3, 5, lovleah, cover (background), OksanaRadchenko, 30–31, PeteMuller, 8, renacal1, 21, tonda, 12–13; Science Source: The Natural History Museum, London, 7; Shutterstock Images: AlessandroZocc, 17, Cathy Keifer, 16, Dudarev Mikhall, 11, 28, EcoPrint, 27, Hue Chee Kong, cover (foreground), MEDIAIMAG, 19, Michaelpuche, 15, Theerawan, 23, Todd Boland, 24–25

Printed in the United States of America.
PA48

TABLE OF CONTENTS

LET'S GET
Growing

Plants make it possible for humans to breathe. They provide medicine to heal people. Plants grow all around the world. There are about 400,000 different **species**. Each type is unique. Each plant is amazing.

The dragon blood tree is found in Yemen, on the Arabian Peninsula.

CHAPTER 2

FLOWER
Power

Flowers are beautiful and colorful. They have been around for millions of years. The oldest known flower lived around 130 million years ago. Scientists found a **fossil** of the flower in Spain. They studied the fossil. The flower lived underwater. It lived among dinosaurs.

Scientists study plant fossils to see what plants were like long ago.

The moon flower is a type of morning glory.

MOONLIGHT ATTRACTION

Most flowers open during the day. Insects fly by. The insects take **pollen** from the flowers. Then the insects spread the pollen to other flowers. But moon flowers open only at night. They usually have large, white blossoms. The blossoms attract insects that come out at night.

SMELLY STALK

The corpse flower is a **rain forest** plant with a big stink. It is a huge **stalk** of many flowers. The corpse flower takes months to grow. Then it starts smelling like rotting flesh. The scent attracts flies. The flies land on the flower. They pick up its pollen. Then they spread the pollen to other plants. Luckily, the smell lasts only a day or two.

CHAPTER 3

AMAZING
Trees

There are more than 23,000 species of trees. The dragon blood tree gives off red **sap**. This "dragon blood" was used as medicine long ago.

Baobab trees look like water bottles. They act like them too. These trees can hold 80 gallons (300 liters) of water!

Baobab trees are found in Africa, the Arabian Peninsula, and Australia.

THE NUMBERS

There are trillions of trees in the world. There are 400 times as many trees as there are humans!

ANCIENT GIANTS

Trees are the longest living organisms in the world. They can live for thousands of years. People count the rings in tree trunks. Each ring means one year of life. A tree in California is more than 5,000 years old!

DO NO HARM

Scientists used to cut down trees to study them. Today scientists use a special tool. They take out a sample of the tree's trunk. They count the rings on the sample.

Some of the oldest
trees in the world are
bristlecone pine trees.

CHAPTER 4

PLANTS FOR
Dinner

Humans have been growing food for thousands of years. They eat fruits and vegetables. They eat cereals. But some plants can be poisonous. People make rhubarb pie from the plant's stalks. But rhubarb leaves are poisonous.

Some vegetables have changed over the years. Most carrots used to be purple. In the 1500s, Dutch farmers bred orange carrots.

People can still find purple carrots today.

Many animals eat plants. Some plants eat animals. A sundew plant has tiny, sticky hairs. These hairs trap flies. The Venus flytrap has an opening like a mouth. It closes around spiders, beetles, or ants. These plants **digest** animals as food.

Venus flytraps
can catch
grasshoppers!

CHAPTER 5

THE DOCTOR
Is In

Plants can be used for medicine. Aspirin is a drug. It helps with pain and fevers. Aspirin was first made from a **compound** in willow bark. Many plants have healing compounds.

One species
of poppy flowers is
used as a painkiller.

Cocoa beans are harvested to make chocolate and cocoa powder.

PLANT MEDICINE

Many medicines first came from plants. These medicines treat allergies. They fight disease. They help with swelling. Some plants make people numb. Other plants wake people up. Coffee and cocoa beans have **caffeine**. Some types of tea leaves do too.

Harvesters let cocoa beans dry in the sun.

CHAPTER 6

MANY
Habitats

Many plants grow in soil. But others grow underwater. Duckweed and watermeal float on water. They don't need soil to grow. They take in **nutrients** from the Sun and water.

Duckweed most often grows on still water, such as lakes or ponds.

Air plants don't grow in soil. They don't grow in water either. They take in nutrients from the air. There are more than 500 species of air plants. They make good houseplants.

The roots of air plants latch on to whatever surface is around them.

Air plants have narrow, grass-like leaves.

CHAPTER 7

DESERT
Plants

The Rose of Jericho is a survivor. It is called the **resurrection** plant. Dry weather makes this plant curl up like a ball. The plant waits for water. Then it uncurls.

The *Welwitschia mirabilis* is one weird plant. It grows in the desert. Its long leaves creep along the sand. It can live to be thousands of years old.

The *Welwitschia mirabilis* plant has only two leaves. They are torn apart by wind over time.

GLOSSARY

caffeine
a chemical that stimulates the nervous system

compound
a chemical made of two or more substances

digest
to break down food

fossil
the image or remains of a living thing that has been preserved in the rock or earth for a very long time

nutrient
a substance that is necessary for survival and growth

pollen
a powdery substance used by flowering plants to spread themselves

rain forest
a dense forest that receives heavy rainfall throughout much of the year

resurrection
the act of coming back to life

sap
a mix of water and minerals that moves through plants

species
a group of plants or animals of the same kind that can produce offspring together

stalk
the main stem of a plant

TRIVIA

1. Black walnut trees produce a toxin. The toxin seeps into the soil. It hurts and sometimes kills nearby plants. Humans and animals are not affected by it.

2. Ripe cranberries bounce and float in water. They have small pockets of air inside. Old cranberries do not float.

3. The world's tallest known tree is a redwood named Hyperion. It towers over the other trees in Redwood National Park in California. It is 379 feet (115 m) tall. That is twice the height of New York City's Statue of Liberty from base to torch!

4. Herbs and spices are both used in cooking. But they are different. Herbs come from the leafy part of a plant. Spices come from a plant's bark, flower, seed, or fruit.

ACTIVITY

GROWING AT HOME

You can grow plants without even leaving your house. Make your own garden using soil, seeds, and clear plastic cups.

1. Add potting soil and vegetable seeds to a clear plastic cup.

2. Set your cup by a window where it will receive a lot of sunlight. Spray in a little water occasionally. Watch the seedling grow.

You can keep a field journal. Record what happens to the plant each day. You can write or draw to describe what you see.

FURTHER RESOURCES

**Ready to learn more about amazing plants?
Check out these books:**

Berger, Melvin. *The Wacky World of Living Things!* New York: Scholastic Inc., 2017.

Slingerland, Janet. *The Secret Lives of Plants!* North Mankato, Minn.: Capstone Press, 2012.

**Want to know more about the science behind plants?
Learn more here:**

DK Find Out!: Plants
www.dkfindout.com/us/animals-and-nature/plants/

Kids Growing Strong: We Love Plants!
https://kidsgrowingstrong.org/we-love-plants/

NASA Climate Kids: Plants and Animals
https://climatekids.nasa.gov/menu/plants-and-animals/

Warwick, Kevin. *What On Earth? Trees.* London, UK: QEB Publishing, 2018.

INDEX